Copyright © 2023 by Todoni Florin
All rights reserved.

No part of this publication may be reproduced, distributed, or transmitted in any form or by any means, including photocopying, recording, or other electronic or mechanical methods, without the prior written permission of the publisher, except in the case of brief quotations embodied in critical reviews and certain other noncommercial uses permitted by copyright law.

100 WEIRD AND INTERESTING FACTS

A Kaleidoscope of Curiosities from Around the Globe

Welcome to "100 Weird and Interesting Facts." In this intriguing collection, we embark on a global journey to unearth some of the most extraordinary, random and weird facts of our world. This collection invites you to dive into a tapestry of fascinating tidbits that span the realms of nature, culture, science, and beyond. From curious phenomena to remarkable historical anecdotes, each fact unveils a new layer of the extraordinary, demonstrating that truth is often stranger than fiction. Prepare to be mesmerized by the captivating facts and surprising truths that make our world an endlessly fascinating place.

Wild Horses will not go to sleep at the same time.

In the wild, where survival is a constant challenge, horses display a remarkable form of teamwork and vigilance. Among a group of horses, it's an unwritten rule that they won't all sleep simultaneously. Instead, they take turns, ensuring that at least one member remains awake and alert to protect the herd from potential threats.

Experiencing 15 minutes of shivering in cold conditions can have the metabolic effect of an entire hour of exercise.

The human body is a marvel of efficiency. One remarkable fact highlights this: just 15 minutes of shivering in cold temperatures can have the same impact on your metabolism as a full hour of exercise. Shivering is your body's way of generating heat to combat the cold. During this involuntary muscular response, your metabolism ramps up, burning calories to keep you warm.

Honey never spoils.

The fact that honey never spoils is a testament to the remarkable longevity of this sweet nectar. Archaeologists have even discovered pots of honey in ancient Egyptian tombs that are over 3,000 years old and still perfectly edible. This exceptional quality is due to honey's low moisture content and high acidity, which create an inhospitable environment for bacteria and microorganisms.

Los Angeles' Milky Way Revelation

In the midst of a major power outage that affected Southern California during the 1990s, something extraordinary happened in Los Angeles. Panicked calls flooded the 911 emergency line, but not for the typical reasons. Residents were bewildered by an unfamiliar sight overhead a tapestry of stars that had long been obscured by the city's luminous glow. What they were actually witnessing was the Milky Way, visible in the night sky.

The Necessity of Ashtrays on Airplanes

In a world where smoking on airplanes has long been prohibited, it may seem counterintuitive to find ashtrays on every plane. However, this seemingly paradoxical feature serves a crucial purpose: safety. Airlines are well aware that some passengers might still break the law. In such cases, the ashtray provides a safe and fireproof means of disposing of the cigarette, preventing any potential fire hazards.

Beards as Body Armor

A study has revealed a rather unexpected function for men's bushy beards. These facial manes aren't just for style – they've evolved to act as a form of natural body armor. Research has shown that beards can soften the impact of punches and provide protection for the delicate jaw underneath. In fact, bearded faces can absorb a staggering 37 percent more energy from a punch compared to their clean-shaven counterparts

Selfies: More Deadly Than Sharks

In the modern age of smartphones and social media, the quest for the perfect selfie has taken a surprising turn. Recent statistics reveal that the pursuit of that ideal self-portrait now results in more fatalities than encounters with one of the ocean's most feared predators, sharks. From risky stunts on cliffs and buildings to dangerous poses near wild animals, the obsession with capturing the perfect selfie has unfortunately led to tragic consequences.

The Great Locust Plague of 1875

In 1875, a cataclysmic event unfolded across the Great Plains when a colossal swarm of Rocky Mountain locusts, numbering a staggering 12.5 trillion, blanketed an astonishing 198,000 square miles. These voracious insects, collectively weighing 27.5 million tons, embarked on a relentless feast, mercilessly consuming every morsel of plant life in their path. The devastation was so profound that farmers attempting to fend off this relentless onslaught often found themselves with clothes devoured right off their bodies.

Tulip Bulbs: The Currency of 17th Century Holland

In the 1600s, a peculiar phenomenon known as "Tulip Mania" swept through Holland. During this extraordinary time, the price of tulip bulbs skyrocketed to astonishing heights, with a single bulb costing more than a grand house. In some cases, tulip bulbs even served as a form of currency. These prized bulbs were sold multiple times, and investors even bought the rights to tulips that had yet to be grown, giving rise to one of history's first futures markets.

Konstanz World War II Light Deception

During World War II, Konstanz a city located near the border between Germany and Switzerland, remained an exceptional anomaly. Rather than adhering to the blackout regulations that most cities enforced to evade Allied bombing raids, Konstanz took a bold approach. The city illuminated itself at night, emulating the radiance of nearby Switzerland. This clever ruse aimed to mislead Allied bomber crews into believing that Konstanz was actually part of Switzerland, sparing it from the destruction that befell so many other German cities during the war.

The Ageless Jellyfish: A Never-Ending Life

In the world of remarkable creatures, a certain type of jellyfish stands out as an extraordinary anomaly. This unique species is known for its remarkable ability to defy the relentless march of time. Unlike most living organisms, these jellyfish don't experience the aging process. In fact, they are considered biologically immortal. They possess the astounding ability to regenerate and rejuvenate their cells, effectively granting them the potential for an eternal existence. Unless met with an untimely demise, these jellyfish will continue to drift through the ocean's currents, unburdened by the inevitable grasp of old age.

A Common Ancestor for All Blue-Eyed People

If you have blue eyes, you're connected to a worldwide family with a shared ancestry. Studies have shown that the genetic mutation responsible for blue eyes can be traced back to a single, common ancestor who lived thousands of years ago. So, every time you lock eyes with another blue-eyed person, remember that you both carry a unique link to the past, connecting you in a subtle yet extraordinary way.

Butterflies in Your Stomach: It's Actually an Adrenaline Rush

The sensation of "butterflies" in your stomach when you're around someone you like is not due to romantic magic, but rather a result of the body's stress response. When you're attracted to someone, your brain releases adrenaline, a hormone that prepares your body for a 'fight or flight' reaction. This surge of adrenaline can lead to that fluttery feeling in your stomach, increased heart rate, and heightened alertness. So, those butterflies are actually your body's way of telling you that it's excited and a little bit on edge!

Generous Parrots

In a remarkable display of empathy and cooperation, researchers taught African grey parrots to use tokens to purchase food. When these clever parrots were paired up, one parrot was given ten tokens, while the other received none. Astonishingly, even without any personal reward, the parrots with tokens willingly shared some of them with their partner who had none, ensuring that everyone had the chance to eat.

Neptune's Pioneering Discovery

Neptune holds the distinction of being the first planet ever discovered through mathematical predictions, a groundbreaking achievement in the field of astronomy. Unlike previous discoveries that relied on telescopes, astronomers Urbain Le Verrier and John Couch Adams, independently and concurrently, used mathematical calculations to predict the existence and position of Neptune. Their precise calculations ultimately led to the observation and confirmation of this distant, enigmatic planet, marking a significant milestone in the history of celestial exploration.

Super Mario's Real-Life Inspiration

Super Mario, the iconic video game character, got his name from a real-life businessman named Mario Segale. Nintendo, in a moment of financial struggle, was renting a warehouse from Segale. When they fell behind on rent, rather than evicting them, Segale gave Nintendo a second chance to make things right. Nintendo managed to recover financially, and in a nod to their landlord's understanding, they named their beloved character after him.

Blue Whales Gargantuan Tongues

The tongues of blue whales, the largest creatures on Earth. On average, a blue whale's tongue is 8 feet (2.5 m) long and weighs around 8,000 pounds (3600 kg), the average size of an adult African elephant. These colossal marine mammals not only impress us with their sheer size but also with this remarkable fact that showcases the incredible scale of nature.

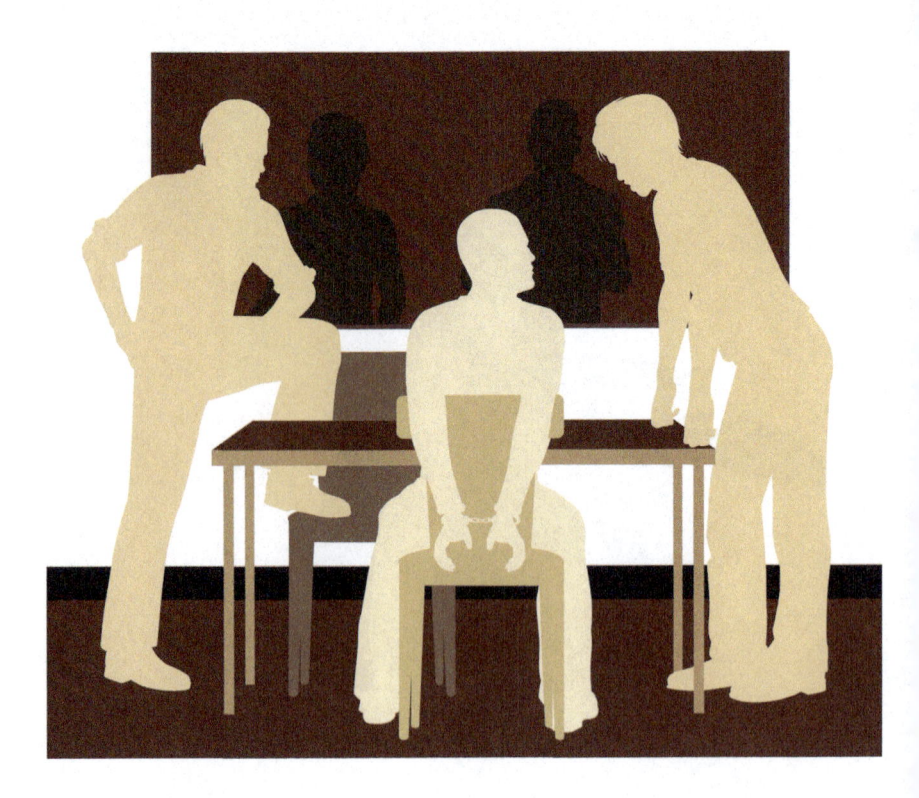

WWII Compassionate Interrogator

Hanns Scharff, a German interrogator during World War II, possessed a unique and humane approach to extracting information from prisoners. Instead of resorting to torture, he created a bond with the captives by sharing jokes, offering homemade meals, and even taking them on peaceful nature walks. Surprisingly, this kind treatment often led prisoners to voluntarily reveal the information Scharff sought, sometimes without even realizing they had done so.

The Spicy Origins of Chocolate

Long before chocolate bars and hot cocoa, the original recipe for chocolate was quite different from what we know today. Instead of being sweet, it contained chili powder, giving it a spicy kick. This unique twist on chocolate reveals how the ancient Mesoamericans enjoyed their cacao-based mixture, adding a flavorful and fiery element to this beloved treat.

Clever Crows

Crows possess an astonishing ability to recognize human faces, a talent that extends beyond mere observation. These intelligent birds can identify and remember individuals who have crossed their path, whether as friends or foes. Remarkably, if you happen to upset a crow, it's a memory they won't soon forget. Moreover, crows have the uncanny knack of warning their fellow crows about a human they deem dangerous, showcasing their social and cognitive prowess in the avian world.

Eiffel Tower Original Destination

The iconic Eiffel Tower, a symbol of Paris and France, wasn't initially destined for the City of Light. In fact, its original intended location was Barcelona, Spain. Designed by engineer Gustave Eiffel, this architectural masterpiece was intended to be the centerpiece of the 1888 Barcelona World's Fair. However, after the proposal was rejected by the city for aesthetic reasons, Eiffel found a new home for his creation in Paris, where it would eventually become one of the most famous landmarks in the world.

The CIA's Secret Heart Attack Gun

In 1975, the CIA unveiled a chillingly covert weapon known as the "Heart Attack Gun" This battery-operated gun fired a tiny dart containing shellfish toxin and frozen water, designed to enter the body, trigger a heart attack, and leave nothing but a small, innocuous red mark at the point of entry. What made it even more sinister was its undetectability in post-mortem examinations, allowing the CIA to carry out assassinations that left no trace.

The Original Thermometer Filling

In a time before the common use of mercury in thermometers, brandy was the unexpected liquid of choice for filling these temperature-measuring instruments. The alcohol's unique properties made it a suitable alternative, with its ability to expand and contract in response to temperature changes. This peculiar historical fact sheds light on the ingenuity of early scientists and the unconventional solutions they devised to advance their understanding of the natural world.

How Men's Brain Processes Voices

The human brain is a complex organ, and the way it processes different types of auditory information can be quite intriguing. When it comes to voices, research has revealed that men process other men's voices using the part of the brain typically reserved for processing simple sounds like car engines and machinery. However, when they hear female voices, it's a different story. The male brain processes female voices in a manner similar to how it processes music.

Dogs Can Be Allergic to Humans!

It may come as a surprise, but just as humans can develop allergies to dogs, dogs can also be allergic to their human companions. These allergies can be triggered by a variety of factors, including human skin cells, saliva, or even the scents we carry on our clothes. While it's not a common occurrence, it's a curious reminder that allergies can affect not only us but our furry friends as well.

Cardiology Conference

A remarkable incident unfolded on a commercial flight when a 67-year-old woman suffered a heart attack. As panic set in, the flight attendant urgently inquired if there was a doctor among the passengers. To everyone's surprise, 15 individuals stood up and offered their help, all of whom were en route to a cardiology conference. With their combined expertise and quick response, they successfully stabilized the woman's condition, ensuring her survival. This heartwarming story serves as a testament to the incredible impact of being in the right place at the right time, surrounded by the right people.

Wimbledon's Swear-Free Zone

In the hallowed courts of Wimbledon, a unique and strict tradition prevails: players are not allowed to swear during matches. To uphold this rule, the line judges must be well-versed in curse words from every corner of the globe, ensuring that no linguistic slip-up goes unnoticed. It's a testament to the tournament's commitment to maintaining an air of decency and sportsmanship on the tennis court.

Babies Secret Mustaches

During fetal development, every unborn baby sprouts a fine layer of hair known as lanugo, which initially appears as a tiny moustache on their upper lip. As the pregnancy progresses, this hair spreads to cover the entire body. Remarkably, the baby doesn't retain this hair after birth; instead, they ingest it while in the womb. Following delivery, the baby expels this hair along with their first bowel movement, known as meconium. It's a strange and fascinating aspect of human development.

Pope Francis: The Former Nightclub Bouncer

Before ascending to the highest position in the Catholic Church, Pope Francis had a rather unexpected job, as a student in Buenos Aires, he worked as a doorman at a nightclub. This intriguing fact reveals the diverse experiences that can shape a person's life, and in his case, it's a testament to the multifaceted journey that led him to become the spiritual leader of millions around the world.

Japanese Forest Therapy

In Japan, doctors often prescribe "Forest Therapy" as a natural remedy for depression and anxiety. The therapeutic practice involves immersing oneself in the forest environment, where the soothing scent of trees has been shown to increase the activity of natural "killer cells." These enhanced immune responses help the body resist stress and contribute to overall mental and physical well-being.

Britney Spears Music scares off Somali Pirates

British Naval Officers found an unconventional way to ward off Somali Pirates off the east coast of Africa in 2013. They discovered that playing Britney Spears' music, such as hits like "Oops! I Did It Again" and "Baby One More Time," had a surprising effect on the pirates. According to one officer, "As soon as the pirates get a blast of Britney, they move on as quickly as they can.

Icelandic App Prevents Cousin Dating

In a unique and light-hearted effort to tackle an unusual social challenge, a group of students at the University of Iceland in Reykjavík designed an Android app that helps Icelanders avoid inadvertently dating their cousins. This innovative app sources its data from the Íslendingabók database, a comprehensive national record containing family trees that stretch back into the Middle Ages. By cross-referencing potential romantic interests with this extensive genealogical resource, the app ensures that Icelanders can pursue relationships with peace of mind, free from the worry of unintended familial connections.

Chimpanzee Experiment Gone Awry

In the 1930s, two psychologists took an unusual approach to study human behavior by adopting a baby chimpanzee and raising her alongside their own infant son, Donald. However, after just nine months, the experiment was abruptly halted because Donald started to behave like a chimpanzee, showing aggression, biting people and even making ape-like noises.

Sloths can hold their breath longer than a dolphin

Sloths can hold their breath for an astonishing 20 minutes, with some individuals even pushing that limit to an astonishing 40 minutes. This remarkable ability is attributed to their unique adaptation of slowing their heart rate to a fraction of its normal pace when submerged. While you might not think of sloths as swimmers, they are, in fact, rather skilled in the water. They use their strong limbs to move with surprising agility and grace. In contrast, dolphins, known for their aquatic prowess, can usually manage only around 10 minutes underwater.

Time Capsule Language - Icelandic's Remarkable Resilience

Iceland's unique geographical isolation has served as a linguistic time capsule, preserving its language in a nearly pristine state. The Icelandic language has undergone minimal changes from its original roots, making it possible for modern Icelanders to read and understand texts written as far back as the 10th century with remarkable ease.

Cows have best friends

Research from the University of Northampton has highlighted the human-like relationships among cattle. Cows, like humans, have a social side to them. They form close bonds with certain companions, and when these bovine best friends are separated, cows can experience real distress and panic. This heartwarming aspect of their social lives reveals the emotional depth and sensitivity of these gentle creatures.

Drunken Bees

In the scorching heat of Australia, an unusual natural phenomenon occurs. When the temperature soars, the nectar within certain flowers ferments and transforms into alcohol. What's even more astonishing is that the bees that collect this fermented nectar may end up getting tipsy from their sweet find. Guard bees stationed at the hive entrance can detect the inebriated state of their fellow workers and prevent them from entering, ensuring that they don't turn the nectar into alcoholic honey.

Ocean Oxygen Production

Surprisingly, roughly half of the oxygen production on Earth doesn't originate from lush forests or towering trees, it comes from the vast oceans. Phytoplankton, tiny marine plants, plays a critical role in this process. Through photosynthesis, they produce a significant portion of the world's oxygen, making the ocean, not just a source of wonder but a literal lifeline for our planet's atmosphere.

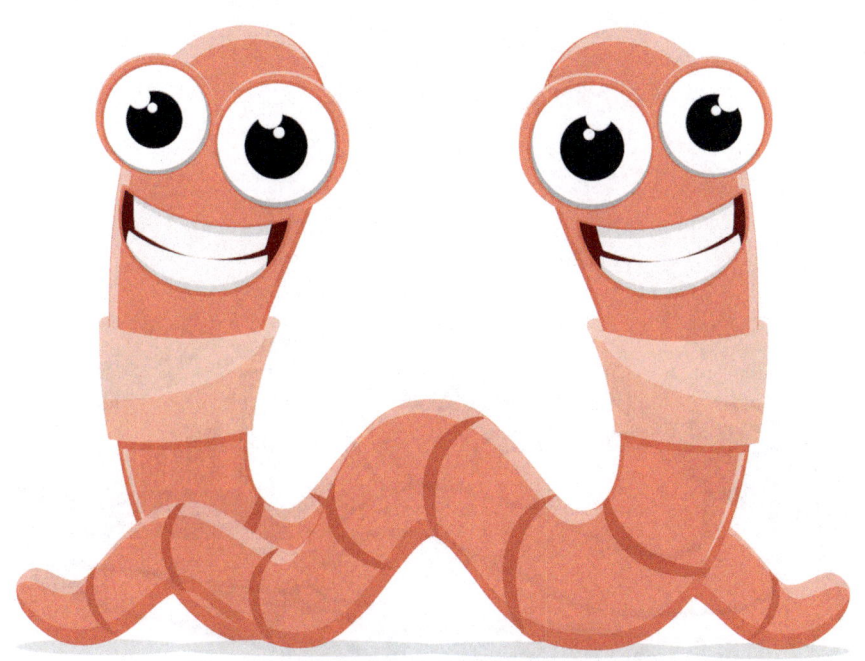

Two-Headed Space Worm

In 2015, scientists conducted a curious experiment by sending flatworms to the International Space Station for a five-week stay to observe how the unique conditions of space would impact their growth. What they discovered was nothing short of astonishing. One of the flatworms emerged from its space sojourn with not one, but two heads! Even more remarkable, when scientists later amputated both heads, each one grew back, underscoring that the effects of space travel had led to a permanent and extraordinary change in the worm's biology.

Japanese Bullet Train Seismometers

The Japanese bullet train system is renowned for its cutting-edge technology and dedication to passenger safety. On March 11, 2011, this commitment to safety was on full display when one of the system's seismometers detected an impending 8.9 magnitude earthquake a mere 12 seconds before it struck. Instantly, a stop signal was relayed to 33 trains, preventing catastrophe and ensuring the safety of countless passengers. Thanks to this remarkable technology, only one bullet train derailed that day.

Fish Eggs Hatching from Duck Droppings

New research reveals an astonishing phenomenon where fish eggs can defy the odds of digestion by surviving their passage through the digestive system of mallard ducks. These resilient eggs exit the ducks in their feces and, upon encountering water again, manage to hatch. This extraordinary adaptation sheds light on the mysterious appearance of fish in ponds and pools without any apparent explanation.

Deafening Dedication

Hiram Maxim, the inventor of the automatic machine gun, was so committed to perfecting his invention that he spent an extensive amount of time test-firing his guns. This relentless pursuit of innovation left him profoundly deaf. In an ironic twist of fate, his son, Hiram Percy Maxim, would later invent the silencer, but it came too late to preserve his father's hearing.

Jaguars' Hallucinogenic Trip

In the lush jungles of South America, a remarkable and little-known behavior has been observed among jaguars. These enigmatic big cats seek out the roots of the caapi plant and gnaw on them until they induce hallucinations. It's a captivating insight into the mysterious world of wildlife, as jaguars, it seems, have a penchant for getting high amidst the verdant forests of South America.

The Red Baron's Honorable Farewell

Even in the heat of battle, there's sometimes room for a touch of humanity. When the renowned World War I flying ace, the "Red Baron" (Manfred von Richthofen), was shot down and killed in combat, his adversaries showed an unusual display of respect. They buried him with full military honors and placed a wreath on his grave that read, "To Our Gallant and Worthy Foe." This remarkable gesture serves as a testament to the mutual respect and chivalry that could exist even in the midst of one of history's deadliest conflicts.

Spiders Venture into the Skies

Despite their lack of wings, spiders possess an extraordinary ability known as "ballooning." By releasing long strands of silk, these intrepid arachnids harness the Earth's air currents and electric fields to embark on epic journeys, sometimes spanning hundreds of miles, including crossing entire oceans. It's a remarkable feat that has led to spiders being discovered as high as two-and-a-half miles above the ground and up to 1,000 miles out at sea.

Lottery Win Turns Tragic

In 1960, an Australian man experienced the joy of winning over $3 million in a lottery, a life-changing stroke of luck. However, his moment of triumph quickly turned into a nightmare when his personal details and images were splashed across the front pages of newspapers. Tragically, his 8-year-old son was kidnapped for ransom and, in a heart-wrenching turn of events, was ultimately murdered. This horrifying incident had a profound impact on Australia, leading to a significant change in anonymity laws for lottery winners, forever altering the way these fortunate individuals could safeguard their privacy.

Genghis Khan's Drastic Command

It is said that Genghis Khan, the legendary Mongol leader, issued a chilling order to his starving troops. They were facing starvation during a long campaign, He commanded that every tenth man should be sacrificed and eaten, as a gruesome means of rationing their limited food supplies. This fact serves as a haunting reminder of the extraordinary measures people throughout history have taken to endure the harshest of circumstances.

Barry Marshall's Self-Experiment

Barry Marshall's groundbreaking discovery that Helicobacter pylori bacteria were responsible for stomach ulcers faced skepticism from the medical community. Unable to test his theory on humans due to ethical restrictions, he took a daring step and drank the bacteria himself. Within days, he developed ulcers, confirming his hypothesis. Marshall subsequently treated the ulcers with antibiotics and, in recognition of his pioneering work, was awarded the Nobel Prize in Physiology or Medicine in 2005.

The Nose-Biting Defense

In 1837, a British man took a rather unusual legal route when he sued a woman for biting off half of his nose. The peculiar twist in this story was that the man's attempt to kiss the woman had not been consensual. However, the judge's ruling turned the tables in a surprising manner. The judge sided with the woman, declaring that, "When a man kisses a woman against her will, she is fully entitled to bite his nose off, if she so pleases."

Chinchilla Fur Thickness

Chinchilla fur is renowned for its incredible softness and thickness, but it possesses a unique quality that's far from common knowledge. This luxurious fur is so dense that any fleas attempting to make a home amidst it will find themselves in an inhospitable environment. The dense chinchilla fur creates an impenetrable barrier, suffocating these tiny pests and preventing them from infesting the adorable rodents.

The A+ Term Paper That Vanished

In 1976, a Princeton junior undergraduate dared to explore the unthinkable in a term paper: "the mechanics of constructing a nuclear bomb". Remarkably, his audacious endeavor earned him an "A" grade, showcasing his academic prowess. However, this academic feat came at a price, as the FBI swiftly seized the paper.

The Enigmatic Dracula Parrot

The Dracula parrot, with its peculiar combination of a parrot's body and a vulture's head, is a truly captivating yet unsettling creature. Its distinctive appearance and vibrant plumage have made it a target of overhunting, driven by high demand in the aviculture industry. As a result, this remarkable species is now listed as "Vulnerable" on the IUCN Red List of Threatened Species.

Sneezing Votes

African wild dogs, known for their complex social structures, have a unique way of making group decisions about whether to go on a hunt. They vote by sneezing. If the dominant pair in the pack initiates the process with a sneeze, it typically takes just two more sneezes from other pack members to signal that a hunt is on the horizon. On the other hand, if non-dominant dogs start the voting process, it may require as many as ten additional sneezes to sway the group's decision in favor of a hunt.

Australia's First Cops

When Australia was established as a penal colony, law and order were essential, but the available manpower was limited to convicts. To maintain some semblance of order, the first police force in Australia was comprised of 12 of the best-behaved convicts, who were tasked with keeping the peace and enforcing the law. In this unusual twist of history, those once labeled as criminals became the keepers of law and order in the new land.

The Quietest Places on Earth

Anechoic chambers are designed to be the quietest places on Earth, with background noises measured in negative decibels. Spending time in these soundproof environments can result in the surreal experience of hearing your own heartbeat and blood circulating in your ears, sometimes causing orientation and balance difficulties.

Astonishing Survival

In a bizarre incident, an Austrian man named Mihavecz found himself unintentionally breaking a record for human endurance. Three police officers inadvertently left him locked in a cell for 18 days, assuming that the others had already released him. Trapped in isolation in the basement, nobody could hear his screams. Mihavecz endured the ordeal without food or liquids, losing a staggering 24 kg (53 pounds) in the process. His harrowing experience serves as a testament to the astonishing resilience of the human body.

Rebuilt Brick by Brick

In 2015, a century-old London pub, The Carlton Tavern, faced an unjust fate at the hands of greedy developers who sought to replace it with something more profitable. However, the story took a remarkable turn when they were ordered to rebuild it precisely as it was, brick by brick, in an act of justice and historical preservation. What makes this tale even more astonishing is that during World War II, when the Blitz ravaged the city, The Carlton Tavern was the sole building on its street that miraculously survived the devastating bombings.

Dogs' MRI Scans Reveal Human Bonds

Recent MRI scans of dogs' brains have unveiled an endearing truth: our furry companions view their owners as family. When presented with various scents, these loyal canines consistently prioritize the smell of humans above all else, providing compelling evidence of the strong emotional connection that exists between dogs and their human counterparts.

Inmates Run Restaurants Open to the Public

In the United Kingdom, a practice exists within the prison system. Several correctional facilities operate restaurants that are entirely staffed by inmates, including chefs and waiters. What's even more remarkable is that these restaurants are open to the public, and surprisingly, some of these prison-run establishments rank highly on platforms like TripAdvisor.

The Pineapple Art in Scotland

At a modern art gallery in Scotland, a clever group of students conducted an unconventional experiment. They placed a humble pineapple in an empty exhibit, curious to see how people would react. When they returned four days later, not only had the pineapple remained undisturbed, but it had also been put on displayed under a protective glass case,

Double-Dealing with the Eiffel Tower

In the 1920s, the notorious con artist Victor Lustig demonstrated his exceptional skill by duping scrap metal dealers into believing that he was a government agent authorized to sell the Eiffel Tower. Lustig concocted a convincing narrative, telling his targets that the iconic Parisian landmark had become too expensive to maintain, and the government had decided to dismantle it. Remarkably, he successfully pulled off this audacious scheme not once, but twice.

Platypus Perplexity

When European scientists first encountered the platypus, they were sceptical. They couldn't believe that such a creature existed. The platypus's unique combination of features, including its egg-laying, duck-like bill, beaver-like tail, otter-like feet, and venomous spurs, seemed like a bizarre concoction. In their skepticism, they assumed it had to be an elaborate hoax, completely unaware that indigenous Aboriginal people had long been aware of this extraordinary mammal. The platypus continues to be a marvel of the animal kingdom, a testament to nature's creativity

Divorce-Reconciliation Room

In the picturesque village of Biertan in Transylvania, Romania, an extraordinary tradition prevailed for centuries. The local church housed a unique room known as the "divorce-reconciliation room." When couples in the village sought to dissolve their marriage, they were required to spend two weeks together in this room, which contained just one small bed, one chair, one table, one plate, and one spoon. The intent was to give couples a chance to reconsider their decision and attempt reconciliation. Surprisingly, over the span of 300 years, this unconventional approach resulted in only a single divorce.

Dutch Families Adopt WWII Graves

In the Netherlands, there's a remarkable cemetery housing the remains of 8,300 US veterans who gave their lives during World War II. What sets this cemetery apart is the heartwarming tradition that has endured for over 70 years. Every Sunday, Dutch families visit the cemetery to care for a grave they have adopted, tending to the resting places of these American heroes. The dedication of these Dutch caretakers is so profound that there are hundreds of people currently on a waiting list to become caretakers.

Queen Balling

In a remarkable display of nature's efficiency, when a queen bee becomes too old or unwell to serve her colony, the worker bees resort to an extraordinary tactic known as "balling." They surround their ailing monarch in a tight cluster, generating heat and effectively raising her body temperature to lethal levels. This unique phenomenon ensures the smooth transition of power within the hive, as a new queen takes the throne and continues the legacy of the hive.

Unmatched Endurance Flight

In 1958, an incredible feat of aviation endurance occurred when two daring pilots achieved the impossible. They embarked on a journey that lasted over two months without landing. What makes this story even more astonishing is that they were able to refuel by matching the speed of a truck driving down a road. To this day, their record remains unbroken

Saving Private Ryan Realism

The opening scene of "Saving Private Ryan" was so realistic that veterans left theaters, considering it the most accurate portrayal of combat they had ever witnessed. The film was so realistic that combat veterans of D-Day and Vietnam left theaters rather than finish watching the opening scene depicting the Normandy invasion. Their visits to posttraumatic stress disorder counselors rose in number after the film's release, and many counselors advised "more psychologically vulnerable" veterans to avoid watching it.

Time-Traveling Birth

In a remarkable twist of time and biology, a frozen embryo that had been conceived in 1992 was brought to life in 2017. Even more astonishing, this frozen embryo was born to a mother who herself had been born in 1991. This intriguing fact highlights the incredible potential of modern reproductive technology to bridge the gaps of time.

The beginning of "Hold Music"

The practice of playing music for callers on hold originated from an accidental occurrence. A loose wire unintentionally turned an office building's steel frame into a massive radio receiver, enabling callers to tune in to local radio stations while they patiently waited on hold.

Point Nemo: The Loneliest Place on Earth

Point Nemo in the southern Pacific Ocean is the most remote location on our planet. Ships passing through this point find themselves an astonishing 2,700 kilometers away from the nearest land, making it one of the most isolated spots on Earth. To put it into perspective, at the right time of day, the closest humans are actually aboard the International Space Station, which orbits approximately 416 kilometers above the Earth's surface.

Luna Moths: A Life Devoted to Love

Adult Luna Moths have a unique life story. They mature without a mouth, and their sole mission during their brief 7-day lifespan is to find a mate. Tragically, they eventually perish from starvation, but their dedication to reproduction is a testament to the wonders of the natural world.

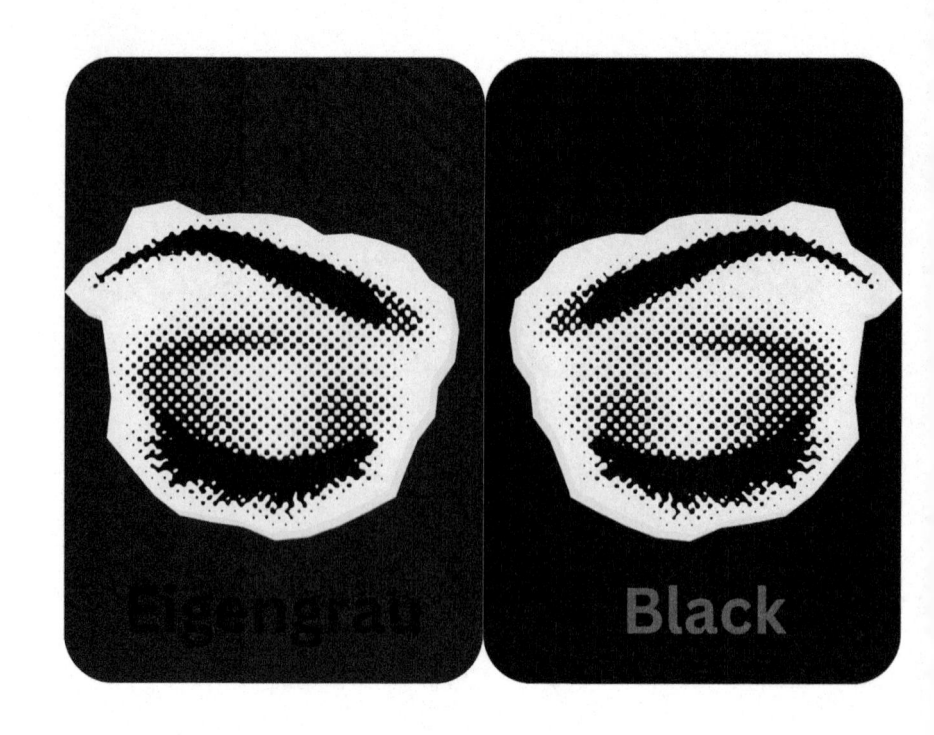

The Color of Closed Eyes

When we close our eyes, we might assume we're seeing darkness or blackness. However, the reality is far more interesting. The color we perceive in the absence of light is called Eigengrau, which translates to "intrinsic gray." Unlike black, which is the absence of all colors, Eigengrau is a unique shade of gray that our brain creates as a result of the constant, low-level activity of our visual receptors

TV Trick: Reducing Bike Shipping Damage

When a Dutch biking company started sending their bikes to the USA, they encountered a significant problem—many of the bikes were arriving damaged. To address this issue, they came up with a creative solution. They began printing an image of an expensive flat-screen television on the cardboard boxes used for shipping. The result? An astonishing 80% decrease in shipping damage, as handlers treated the packages with greater care, thinking they contained delicate electronics.

Riding Across the US in Pants

In 1916, Adeline and Augusta Van Buren embarked on an extraordinary journey across the United States on two solo motorcycles. Their remarkable adventure was not without its challenges; they defied societal norms of the time and frequently found themselves arrested for wearing pants. Despite the obstacles they faced, these pioneering women left an indelible mark on history, challenging gender stereotypes and paving the way for future generations of female adventurers.

Rapid Rodent Reproduction

In the right conditions, a pair of rats can reproduce so prolifically that in just three years, they can give rise to a staggering population of 482 million rats. This astounding rate of reproduction highlights the incredible adaptability and resilience of these small mammals.

A Trust Betrayed

In 2007, a heartwarming tradition turned into a shocking heist in Antwerp, Belgium. An elderly man had been regularly visiting a local bank, bearing sweets and gifts for the staff. His consistent kindness earned him the trust of every member of the bank. So much so that he was granted unsupervised access to their vaults. However, this seemingly benevolent visitor had other plans. Once he gained their trust, he made off with a staggering 120,000 carats of jewels, valued at over 28 million dollars, leaving the bank and its staff in disbelief.

Bunkers for the People

Switzerland's meticulous approach to emergency preparedness is nothing short of astonishing. The country has built bunkers capable of accommodating 114% of its population, ensuring that in times of crisis, there is a secure place for everyone. This level of foresight exemplifies Switzerland's commitment to safeguarding its citizens.

Binaural Beats

Binaural beats are a unique form of auditory stimulation where two slightly different frequencies are presented separately to each ear. This auditory trickery has been reported to induce altered states of consciousness and even trigger unusually vivid and immersive dreams. While scientific research on the topic is ongoing, the potential for binaural beats to offer listeners a gateway to intriguing mental experiences is a fascinating subject of study and exploration.

Quiet When It Snows

When fresh snow blankets the earth, it acts as a natural sound absorber, creating a serene hush over the landscape. This phenomenon occurs because the tiny air pockets trapped between snowflakes dampen vibrations, effectively lowering ambient noise. As a result, when it snows, the world seems to embrace a peaceful stillness, offering a unique and tranquil auditory experience.

Ravens and Wolves

Common ravens have demonstrated an astonishing behavior by calling wolves to the location of dead animals. When the wolves arrive, they open the carcass, making the leftovers more easily accessible to the ravens. This intriguing example of cooperation between two very different species highlights the intricate web of interactions in the animal kingdom.

Lawyer's experiment gone wrong

In a bizarre and tragic incident that unfolded in 1993, a lawyer in Toronto embarked on a perilous experiment to demonstrate the "unbreakable" nature of a 24th-floor window. Despite successfully executing this stunt twice before, his third attempt ended in disaster. Instead of shattering, the glass unexpectedly popped out of its frame, causing him to plummet to his death.

A Family Photo on the Moon

During the Apollo 16 mission on April 23, 1972, astronaut Charlie Duke left a unique memento on the lunar surface. A family photo was carefully placed on the Moon's rocky terrain. On the back of this photograph, a message was inscribed: "This is the family of astronaut Charlie Duke from planet Earth who landed on the moon on April 20, 1972."

Guinea Pig Loneliness Law

Switzerland has a unique law that prohibits owning a single guinea pig. This regulation stems from the understanding that guinea pigs are highly social creatures and can become lonely when kept alone. To ensure their well-being, Swiss law mandates that these furry rodents must have a companion to keep them company.

Hatpins: Unconventional Weapons

In the early 1900s, women wielded hatpins as more than just fashion accessories. These sharp and ornate pins became tools of self-defense against street harassment. They proved so effective that they not only protected women but also symbolized female empowerment. This phenomenon was so significant that it prompted legislative attempts to regulate the length and use of hatpins, as some men experienced painful encounters with these unconventional weapons.

The Remarkable Railroad Baboon

In the late 1800s, an extraordinary story unfolded in the world of railroads. A baboon was employed as a signalman, and remarkably, he never made a single mistake throughout his career. This unusual but true tale stands as a testament to the unexpected ways in which humans and animals can collaborate in the most unconventional of roles. The baboon's dedication and competence earned him a place in railroad history, where he worked faithfully until the end of his days.

Langholm's Legacy

The famed astronaut Neil Armstrong, the first person to set foot on the moon, found himself in Langholm, Scotland, in 1972. During his visit, he was presented with a 400-year-old law that declared any individual with the last name "Armstrong" found in the town should face the grim punishment of hanging.

Babirusa's Lethal Tusks

The Babirusa, a wild pig species found in parts of Southeast Asia, is known for a bizarre and fatal quirk. In particular, the males of this species develop tusks that grow so long they ultimately curve backward and, astonishingly, impale their own skulls. This gruesome natural feature can lead to a slow and painful demise for the unfortunate Babirusa, serving as a stark example of the peculiar and sometimes brutal aspects of the animal kingdom.

Swallowed AirPod

A Taiwanese man unwittingly ingested an Apple AirPod while he was fast asleep. When he awoke, he hit Apple's tracking and heard beeps coming from inside his body. He immediately sought medical attention at the hospital, where a confirmed diagnosis revealed the earbud's location in his stomach. Astonishingly, the AirPod passed through his system naturally. After a thorough wash and drying, the resilient device not only survived but continued to function normally, with its battery still holding a remarkable 41%.

An Apple a Day

The incredible diversity of apple varieties is truly mind-boggling. With thousands of apple types across the globe, each offering a unique taste and texture, it would take you more than 20 years of daily apple consumption to sample them all.

Salty Potatoes

In Japan, an intriguing observation was made when a group of monkeys exhibited a surprising culinary preference. These intelligent primates initially learned to wash sweet potatoes in fresh water to clean them, but over time, they transitioned to washing the tubers in saltwater. The prevailing theory suggests that their shift in behavior may be driven by their fondness for the salty taste, which adds an intriguing twist to their dietary habits.

Fictional Characters

While fictional characters may exist only in the realms of imagination, our connections with them are undeniably real. Research indicates that our brains struggle to differentiate between our familiarity with TV characters and our personal relationships with actual individuals. This phenomenon is so potent that simply contemplating watching our favorite TV show can alleviate feelings of loneliness.

Endless Shores Down Under

Australia boasts a staggering number of over 10,000 beaches, a coastal paradise that beckons exploration. If one were to visit a new beach every day, the adventure would span over 27 years. Vast coastal wonders waiting to be discovered along the sun-kissed shores of Australia.

A victim of his own creation

Sir Robert Watson-Watt, the brilliant mind behind RADAR, found himself in an ironic twist when he was caught speeding using a RADAR gun. Reportedly, he humorously remarked, "My God, if I'd known what they were going to do with it, I'd have never have invented it!"

Sea Wolves of British Columbia

In the coastal wilderness of British Columbia, a unique breed of wolves, aptly named "sea wolves or coastal wolves," has adapted to a life intertwined with the ocean. These remarkable canines defy conventional wolf behavior, swimming several miles each day in pursuit of their primary food source. Astoundingly, up to 90 percent of their diet is sourced from the sea.

Drawings mistaken for photographs.

Renowned artist H.R. Giger, famed for designing the iconic alien in the "Alien" movie, found himself in an amusing predicament when Dutch customs mistook his eerie drawings for actual photographs. In response, Giger humorously questioned, "Where on Earth did they think I could have photographed my subjects? In hell, perhaps?"

The Torre Mayor

The Torre Mayor in Mexico stands tall as the third tallest building in the country, but its true marvel lies in its extraordinary earthquake resistance. Designed to endure earthquakes measuring up to 8.5 on the Richter Scale, this architectural masterpiece proved its mettle in 2003 when a 7.6 magnitude earthquake shook the city. Astonishingly, the Torre Mayor remained unscathed, leaving both the building and its occupants unaware of the seismic event that occurred around them.

Rewatching Favorite Movies

Indulging in the habit of watching your favorite movies repeatedly isn't just a pastime; it's a form of therapeutic escape. The repetition brings a sense of calmness, providing a reassuring familiarity in an otherwise unpredictable world. Knowing the outcome of the story creates a feeling of safety, and the experience can be comforting as it revives and recaptures emotions and moments that may have been lost or overlooked.

Poseidon's Kiss

Ever wondered about the phenomenon when water splashes up from the toilet as your poop drops in? There's a quirky term for it – 'Poseidon's Kiss.' This whimsical expression adds a touch of humor to a common yet peculiar bathroom occurrence, connecting it to the mythical god of the sea who, in this context, seems to playfully greet you from the depths of the toilet bowl.

A Hero's Sacrifice

In 2011, during the Tohuku earthquake and tsunami in Japan, 24-year-old Miki Endo emerged as a hero. Working at the Crisis Management Department in Minamisanriku town, she valiantly broadcasted warnings through loudspeakers, aiding thousands in evacuating to safety. Tragically, her bravery knew no bounds, as she continued her life-saving efforts until the waves engulfed her office, claiming her life in the process.

The Double Tree

Nestled near Piemonte, Italy, the 'Double Tree of Casorzo' is no ordinary tree. It boasts a rare and fascinating union, a cherry tree flourishing atop a mulberry tree. This natural marvel exemplifies the harmonious coexistence of two distinct trees, creating a botanical spectacle that defies conventional expectations.

CONTENTS:

Wild Horses Teamwork..........................3
15 Minutes of Shivering.........................4
Honey Never Spoils..............................5
Milky Way Revelation...........................6
Ashtrays on Airplanes..........................7
Beards as Body Armor.........................8
Selfies are Deadly................................9
The Great Locust Plague.....................10
Tulip Bulbs Currency...........................11
World War II Light Deception...............12
The Ageless Jellyfish...........................13
Blue-Eyed Common Ancestor.............14
Butterflies in Your Stomach.................15
Generous Parrots...............................16
Neptune's Pioneering Discovery...........17
Super Mario's Inspiration....................18
Blue Whales Tongues.........................19
Compassionate Interrogator................20
The Spicy Origins of Chocolate............21
Clever Crows.....................................22
Eiffel Tower Original Destination..........23
Heart Attack Gun...............................24
Thermometer Filling...........................25

How Men's Brain Processes Voices.........26
Dogs Allergic to Humans.....................27
Cardiology Conference.......................28
Wimbledon's Swear-Free Zone.............29
Babies Secret Mustaches....................30
Pope Francis The Nightclub Bouncer.......31
Japanese Forest Therapy....................32
Music scares off Pirates.....................33
Icelandic App Prevents Incest..............34
Chimpanzee Experiment Gone Awry........35
Sloths VS Dolphins............................36
Time Capsule Language......................37
Cows have best friends.....................38
Drunken Bees..................................39
Oxygen Production...........................40
Two-Headed Space Worm....................41
Japanese Bullet Train Seismometers........42
Fish Eggs from Duck Droppings.............43
Deafening Dedication........................44
Jaguars' Hallucinogenic Trip.................45
Red Baron's Honorable Farewell............46
Spiders Venture into the Skies..............47
Lottery Win Turns Tragic.....................48
Genghis Khan's Drastic Command.........49

Barry Marshall's Self-Experiment............50
The Nose-Biting Defense......................51
Chinchilla Fur Thickness......................52
The A+ Term Paper That Vanished...........53
The Enigmatic Dracula Parrot.................54
Sneezing Votes...................................55
Australia's First Cops..........................56
The Quietest Places on Earth.................57
Astonishing Survival............................58
Rebuilt Brick by Brick..........................59
Dogs' MRI Scans Reveal Human Bonds...60
Inmates Run Restaurants......................61
The Pineapple Art in Scotland................62
Double-Dealing with the Eiffel Tower......63
Platypus Perplexity.............................64
Divorce-Reconciliation Room.................65
Dutch Families Adopt WWII Graves........66
Queen Balling....................................67
Unmatched Endurance Flight.................68
Saving Private Ryan Realism..................69
Time-Traveling Birth............................70
The beginning of "Hold Music"..............71
The Loneliest Place on Earth.................72
Luna Moths: A Life Devoted to Love........73

The Color of Closed Eyes......................74
Reducing Bike Shipping Damage............75
Riding Across the US in Pants.................76
Rapid Rodent Reproduction...................77
A Trust Betrayed...................................78
Bunkers for the People..........................79
Binaural Beats......................................80
Quiet When It Snows............................81
Ravens and Wolves...............................82
Lawyer's experiment gone wrong............83
A Family Photo on the Moon..................84
Guinea Pig Loneliness Law.....................85
Hatpins: Unconventional Weapons.........86
The Remarkable Railroad Baboon............87
Langholm's Legacy...............................88
Babirusa's Lethal Tusks.........................89
Swallowed AirPod.................................90
An Apple a Day....................................91
Salty Potatoes......................................92
Fictional Characters..............................93
Endless Shores Down Under...................94
A victim of his own creation...................95
Sea Wolves of British Columbia..............96
Drawings mistaken for photographs........97

The Torre Mayor..................................98
Rewatching Favorite Movies...................99
Poseidon's Kiss..................................100
A Hero's Sacrifice...............................101
The Double Tree.................................102

CREDITS:

All images were provided by:

www.canva.com
Wikipedia

Facts are obtained from various sources of public news media.

Author:
Todoni Florin

Printed in Great Britain
by Amazon